CL

EXTREME WEATHER AND CLIMATE CHANGE

What's the Connection?

Stuart A. Kallen

ReferencePoint Press®

San Diego, CA

About the Author

Stuart A. Kallen is the author of more than 350 nonfiction books for children and young adults. He has written on topics ranging from the theory of relativity to the art of electronic dance music. In 2018 Kallen won a Green Earth Book Award from the Nature Generation environmental organization for his book *Trashing the Planet: Examining the Global Garbage Glut*. In his spare time, he is a singer, songwriter, and guitarist in San Diego.

For more information, contact:
ReferencePoint Press, Inc.
PO Box 27779
San Diego, CA 92198
www.ReferencePointPress.com

Picture Credits:
Cover: Shutterstock.com
 5: Rixipix/iStock
 9: fotomak/Shutterstock.com
11: S. Pech/Shutterstock.com
19: Anna LoFi/Shutterstock.com
23: Cathy Withers-Clarke/Shutterstock.com
28: Associated Press
31: Shane Greckel/Shutterstock.com
33: Sourabh_Vyas/Shutterstock.com
38: Leonard Zhukovsky/Shutterstock.com
40: elRoce/Shutterstock.com
43: Joel Mataro/ZUMA Press/Newscom
47: Drone Dood/Shutterstock.com
52: Associated Press

LIBRARY OF CONGRESS CATALOGING-IN-PUBLICATION DATA

Names: Kallen, Stuart A., 1955- author.
Title: Extreme weather and climate change: what's the connection? / Stuart A. Kallen.
Description: San Diego, CA : ReferencePoint Press, 2022. | Includes bibliographical references and index.
Identifiers: LCCN 2020056595 (print) | LCCN 2020056596 (ebook) | ISBN 9781678200800 (library binding) | ISBN 9781678200817 (ebook)
Subjects: LCSH: Climatic extremes--Juvenile literature. | Climatic changes--Juvenile literature.
Classification: LCC QC981.8.C53 K35 2022 (print) | LCC QC981.8.C53 (ebook) | DDC 363.34/92--dc23
LC record available at https://lccn.loc.gov/2020056595
LC ebook record available at https://lccn.loc.gov/2020056596

CONTENTS

The Climate Is Changing

For those who study climate, September 2020 stood out for a number of reasons. The month was the hottest September on record, and the year was on track to be the hottest since records were first kept in 1880. The sweltering temperatures were blamed for extreme weather in the United States, Europe, Asia, and elsewhere. In California a combination of drought and record heat sparked mega wildfires in mid-August that had consumed a record 1 million acres (404,686 ha) by the end of September. This was three times more than the previous record, set only in 2018. And by the end of November, another 3 million acres (1.2 million ha) of California had burned.

Extreme heat was not the only dire weather news in September. At the other end of the spectrum, temperatures in the northern plains plunged 55°F (31°C) in one day, bringing a rapid end to the growing season a month sooner than usual. In the southeastern United States, tropical storms and hurricanes resulted in record-breaking winds, rain, and floods that left large swaths of Florida, Texas, and Alabama underwater. The story was much the same in China, India, and East Africa, where an unprecedented surge of floods and storms disrupted lives and destroyed croplands and natural habitat.

The disasters that occurred in September 2020 were part of a pattern of extreme weather blamed on climate change, or what author and University of California, Berkeley, lecturer Mark Schapiro calls "climate Volatility, with a capital V."[1] Schapiro says the weather went haywire as natural disasters that were once rare became increasingly commonplace.

Scientists say the upsurge in volatile weather is caused by a rapidly heating climate that is a direct result of fossil fuel consumption. When people burn coal, gas, and oil, they pump planet-warming gases like carbon dioxide (CO_2) and methane into the atmosphere. This has caused average temperatures on earth to warm nearly 2°F (1°C) in the past two centuries. While two degrees does not sound like much, the rising temperatures have upset the balance of nature. Warmer temperatures are causing sea ice to melt at the earth's poles, creating habitat loss for polar bears, seals, seabirds, and other animals. Climate change is a factor behind major droughts and massive wildfires in the American West and Australia. Warming oceans are causing bigger and deadlier rainstorms, hurricanes, and floods affecting millions in areas from the Midwest to the Philippines. As wildfire fighter and climate researcher Jordan Thomas explains, "Several generations of fossil fuel emissions have produced higher atmospheric carbon

Warmer temperatures at the earth's poles are causing sea ice to melt, resulting in habitat loss for animals such as polar bears.

concentrations than have existed at any point in human history. Scientists are certain that the majority of current climatic extremes are the result of this rapid carbon influx. Scientists are also certain that the effects of climate change are catastrophic right now . . . around the world."[2]

"Scientists are . . . certain that the effects of climate change are catastrophic right now . . . around the world."[2]

—Jordan Thomas, climate researcher

The number of catastrophes is expected to grow because the planet continues to get hotter; nine of the ten warmest years on record have occurred since 2005. According to a 2020 report by the United Nations Office for Disaster Risk Reduction (UNDRR), climate change is to blame for more than seventy-three hundred extreme weather–related disasters that have occurred in the twenty-first century. These disasters have killed more than 1.2 million people and cost more than $3 trillion. As the UNDRR report concludes, "It is baffling that we willingly and knowingly continue to sow the seeds of our own destruction, despite the science and evidence that we are turning our only home into an uninhabitable hell for millions of people."[3]

CHAPTER 1

Intense Heat

The Siberian region in northern Russia has long been associated with brutally cold winters. And the Siberian town with the tongue-twisting name of Verkhoyansk is known as a "Pole of Cold" in the Northern Hemisphere. This name is given to places where the lowest temperatures on earth have been recorded. Verkhoyansk earned the Pole of Cold title in February 1892, when the thermometer dipped to -90°F (-68°C). Even in years when records are not being broken, Verkhoyansk is one of the coldest inhabited places on earth. Average January temperatures in the small village are close to -50°F (-45°C).

In June 2020 Verkhoyansk set another weather record. During an unprecedented heat wave, local thermometers registered a sweltering 100.4°F (38°C). The extreme heat, called bizarre by climatologists, continued for a week. Daily temperature records kept since 1885 were broken. People in Verkhoyansk hung blankets over their windows to keep out the heat. Some reported skin conditions and headaches related to the hot weather. Local fishers also suffered; while fish are normally plentiful in local lakes and rivers, they became harder to catch when they swam down deep into colder waters. As local scientist Roman Desyatkin said, "Very strange things are happening here. . . . Our plants, our animals and our people are not used to such great heat."[4]

Blaming Climate Change

An occasional hot summer day is not unusual in Verkhoyansk; the town is located just north of the Arctic Circle, where the sun shines twenty-four hours a day in the summer. But the record-setting heat followed an unusually warm, snowless winter and the hottest-ever spring when temperatures were 20°F (11°C) above normal. While the extreme heat might have shocked local residents, it was not surprising to scientists. As climatologist Ruth Mottram stated, "For a long time, we've been saying we're going to get more extremes like strong heat waves. . . . The projections are coming true, and sooner than we might have thought."[5]

The extreme heat generated interest among scientists in Germany, who wanted to determine what caused the heat wave. The scientists studied weather models and historical information, which led them to conclude that the Verkhoyansk heat wave was made six hundred times more likely as a result of human-induced climate change. As environmental journalist Alejandra Borunda explains, the record Siberian heat is "a signal of a rapidly and continually warming planet, and a preview of how Arctic warming will continue in an increasingly hot future."[6]

The warming planet is pushing up temperatures far beyond remote villages in Siberia. Average summer temperatures in 2020 were the highest ever recorded around the globe, according to the National Oceanic and Atmospheric Administration (NOAA), a US science agency. At least fifty other cities worldwide set records for extreme heat in Southeast Asia, South America, North America, and elsewhere. In August the temperature in California's Death Valley National Park reached 130.4°F

"We've been saying we're going to get more extremes like strong heat waves. . . . The projections are coming true, and sooner than we might have thought."[5]

—Ruth Mottram, climatologist

"[The Siberian heat wave is] a signal of a rapidly and continually warming planet, and a preview of how Arctic warming will continue in an increasingly hot future."[6]

—Alejandra Borunda, environmental journalist

Temperatures in Death Valley National Park are often very hot in the summer, but in August of 2020 a reading of 130.4°F (54.7°C) was reached— the highest ever reliably recorded on earth.

Death Valley National Park

Homeland of the Timbisha Shoshone

(54.7°C). While this desert region is often very hot in the summer, that record-setting temperature was the highest ever reliably recorded on earth.

Heat Kills

The five hottest years recorded on earth have all occurred since 2015. This warming follows a sixty-year trend; every decade since the 1960s has been hotter than the previous ten-year period. And while heat waves are a natural occurrence, the number of extended periods of extreme heat is increasing at an alarming rate. In 1960 the fifty largest cities in the United States experienced an average of two heat waves each summer. By 2020 that number had tripled to six, according to the Adrienne Arsht–Rockefeller Foundation Resilience Center. And heat waves often have deadly consequences.

Heat waves sicken people by causing what is called heat exhaustion, a condition marked by excessive sweating, nausea, headaches, dizziness, weakness, and extreme thirst. If left untreated,

The Permafrost Is Melting

Arctic heat waves are doing more than creating new entries for the record books. The snow that historically covers the Arctic Circle most of the year plays a crucial role in keeping the entire planet cool. The bright, white snow reflects the heat of the sun back into space like a mirror. But as the climate has warmed, the snow has begun melting earlier in the spring and accumulating later in the fall. This heat is melting the frozen layer of soil called permafrost, which makes up about 25 percent of the Northern Hemisphere and about 85 percent of Alaska, Greenland, Canada, and Siberia.

Permafrost is a mixture of soil, rocks, and ice. It also holds four times more CO_2 than humanity has produced in the past two hundred years. As climate change accelerates, the permafrost is melting at an astonishing rate. Scientists estimate that around 40 percent of the Arctic permafrost will melt by the end of the century, with dire consequences. Huge amounts of CO_2 that have been locked up in the permafrost for millennia will be released into the atmosphere. This will further heat the planet, creating conditions that will increase the number of heat waves in the future.

heat exhaustion leads to heatstroke as body temperatures increase to 104°F (40°C) or more. One of the first symptoms of heatstroke is mental confusion, which often leaves victims unaware of what is happening to them. As the body temperature rises, vital organs shut down, including the heart, kidneys, and brain. Kathy Baughman McLeod of the Adrienne Arsht–Rockefeller Foundation Resilience Center calls heat waves "silent killers"[7] because the deaths largely occur among society's most vulnerable people—the very young, the elderly, the poor, and those who have chronic medical conditions such as diabetes, heart disease, and respiratory illnesses. People who live in urban areas—and lack access to air-conditioning—are most often victims of heatstroke. According to the Centers for Disease Control and Prevention, more than six hundred people in the United States die every year due to heat-related illnesses.

In 2003 Europe experienced one of the deadliest heat waves on record. An extended period of heat through July and August killed more than seventy thousand people in the United Kingdom, Spain,

Italy, Germany, and elsewhere. An estimated fifteen thousand of those deaths occurred in France. Most of the victims were elderly. In the summer of 2019, another heat wave spread across Europe. In July of that year, thermometers in Montpellier, a small village in southern France, topped 114.6°F (45.9°C), the highest temperature ever recorded in France. French winemaker Jerome Despey said his vines looked like they were scorched with a blowtorch: "I've been a winegrower for 30 years. I have never seen a vine burnt by a sudden onset of heat."[8] Temperature records were also broken in Bulgaria, Portugal, Italy, Greece, and elsewhere. Authorities were better prepared for the heat this time. Air-conditioned "cooling rooms" were opened in many areas, schools were closed, and public pools stayed open for extended hours. Despite the precautions, around fifteen hundred people died from heat-related illness in France, and a similar number were stricken in the United Kingdom.

Heat waves can be even more deadly in developing nations, where those sickened by heat-related illnesses have fewer resources like medical care, clean water, and adequate food. And

People wade in fountains at the foot of the Eiffel Tower in Paris. An extended heat wave in 2003 killed an estimated fifteen thousand people in France.

the problem is expected to grow. According to the World Health Organization, an increase in the number of heat waves is predicted to cause approximately 250,000 additional deaths per year between 2030 and 2050.

Changes in the Jet Streams

The growing number of heat waves can be traced to changes in the jet streams—fast-moving currents of air that shape weather patterns around the world. There are two dominant jet streams in the Northern Hemisphere; the northernmost polar jet stream is close to the Arctic Circle, while the subtropical jet stream is near the equator. The Southern Hemisphere also has a polar and a subtropical jet stream.

The polar jet stream exerts a strong influence on weather in the United States, Canada, and Europe. This powerful, high-altitude wind in the stratosphere 5 to 7 miles (8 to 11 km) above earth travels from west to east at speeds of up to 200 miles per hour (322 kph). The jet stream naturally flows in a fairly straight pattern parallel to the equator, moving to the north or south depending on the season. However, the traditional flow of the jet stream is being interrupted due to climate change. The wind currents sometimes develop kinks, coiling into previously unseen patterns and snaking from far north to far south. According to science writer Brian Kahn, the problem could be due to melting ice and snow far to the north: "An increasingly kinky jet stream has to do with rapid Arctic warming, which is reducing the temperature [variable] that usually pulls the jet stream taut between the Arctic and [regions to the south]."[9] When the jet stream wavers, it slows down. This can result in a blocking event, which is when the jet stream gets stuck in a harmful pattern for an extended period of time. A blocking event can hold high pressure, or clear skies and warm temperatures, in one place for weeks or months. It can also do the reverse, keeping low pressure systems in one place and causing extensive rain and flooding.

Meteorologists blamed changes in natural jet stream patterns for the stubborn heat wave that set thermometers soaring in Europe in 2019. The heat was caused by a jet stream that coiled up over the North Atlantic, dipping abruptly south before taking a sharp turn north. The unusually contorted jet stream cut off cooler air from the north while allowing hot desert air from Africa to flow up to the European continent.

Increased Demand for Air-Conditioning

When heat waves occur, air-conditioning can lower the number of heat-related deaths. However, air conditioners are power-hungry machines that use more electricity than other household appliances. According to Silicon Valley Power, a single-room air conditioner uses as much energy per hour as four refrigerators or twenty-three large-screen televisions. During a 2018 heat wave in Beijing, China, 50 percent of all electricity being generated was used to run air conditioners.

The high demand for cool air during hot spells is stressing the power grid in many places. During the record-breaking heat wave in California in August 2020, hundreds of thousands of people were left without power as demand for electricity surged and overworked equipment broke down. Power blackouts are dangerous when temperatures soar and people are left without any means to cool off.

The high demand for electricity during heat spells is also creating what is known as a feedback loop. When more people run air conditioners, it increases the amount of pollution generated by power plants that use coal, natural gas, and oil. That in turn increases the amount of CO_2 in the atmosphere, further aggravating the problem of climate change. A headline in *Science* magazine succinctly defined the climate change feedback loop: "The Hotter It Gets, the Hotter It Gets."[10]

The feedback loop is expected to accelerate as the planet continues to warm and the number of air conditioners increases. According to the International Energy Agency, there were around 1 billion air-conditioning units worldwide in 2020. By 2050 that number is expected to increase to 4.5 billion. The agency says that the electricity needed to power these air conditioners will worsen climate change, producing an extra 2.2 billion tons (2 billion metric tons) of CO_2 annually.

Too Hot for Humanity

Scientists warn that the world is going to get even hotter unless people drastically reduce the amount of CO_2 and other climate-warming gases they have been pumping into the atmosphere. Without big changes, scientists say, parts of South Asia will be too hot for human habitation by 2100. The regions that are likely to feel the most devastating effects—northern India, Bangladesh, and southern Pakistan—are home to more than 1.5 billion people. Many of the people in these developing nations are subsistence farmers, who work long hours outdoors on small plots of land where they grow only enough food for basic survival. When extreme hot weather hits, they have no choice but to continue their labors.

South Asia is already one of the warmest regions on earth, and it is also very humid. The combination of high heat and high humidity creates what is called a heat index, or a "feels like" temperature. For example, when the air temperature is 94°F (34.4°C) combined with 80 percent humidity, it feels like 129°F (54°C) on the NOAA Heat Index. The body cools itself by sweating; heat is removed from the body when perspiration evaporates. When the heat index is very high, evaporation slows. This can cause the body to dangerously overheat. Those who live in rural areas of South Asia have few ways to cope with the growing number of days with extreme heat. Thousands are already on the move, migrating to cities in search of food, water, and air-conditioned buildings.

"Reducing our carbon emissions now will really make a difference in the future."[11]

—Richard Rood, climate expert

Extreme heat indexes are not just a problem in developing nations. In the United States numerous cities—including New Orleans, St. Louis, Chicago, and Cleveland—are experiencing longer periods of heat and humidity in the summer. And according to a 2020 study by the National Academy of Sciences, without drastic cuts in CO_2 emissions, people living in the largest US cities will experience twenty times more exposure to extreme heat by the end of the century. While human behavior is driving extreme weather, human behavior can also lessen the damage. As climate expert Richard Rood says, "Reducing our carbon emissions now will really make a difference in the future."[11]

CHAPTER 2

Deadly Droughts and Gigafires

Australia is one of the most fire-prone places in the world. The nation's natural environment was sculpted over millions of years by wildfires that periodically swept through the region. Giant eucalyptus trees depend on these fires to trigger seed production and burn up underbrush that competes for water and minerals in the soil.

While wildfires have long been a regular occurrence in Australia, fire-tolerant plants only thrive when wildfires break out about once every twenty-five years. This was the pattern during the twentieth century, when there were four major wildfires in Australia. But the warming climate is changing the equation; there have already been five major wildfires in Australia since the beginning of the twenty-first century. Some forest ecosystems have collapsed completely, threatening endangered plants and animals with extinction.

Australia's most devastating wildfires broke out in September 2019 after three years of severe drought, and during a month when temperatures averaged 18°F (10°C) above normal in some regions. The fires were ignited by dry lightning—lightning that was not part of a rainstorm. Extreme low humidity and gusty winds quickly spread the flames, making them impossible for firefighters to extinguish. In January 2020 National Aeronautics and Space Administration (NASA) satellites detected more than 1 million separate fires burning across the Australian continent, ranging from small isolated flames to megafires burning on a scale never before seen.

The disastrous wildfires burned largely out of control until March 2020. Australians referred to this period as the Black Summer. (The nation is located in the Southern Hemisphere, and these fires occurred during Australia's warm summer season.) By the time the Black Summer ran its course, over 46 million acres (18.6 million ha) had burned.

Around one-third of the fires occurred in brush and eucalyptus forests in the state of New South Wales. The smoke from the wildfires was so thick that life ground to a halt in Sydney, Australia's largest city. The smoke triggered fire alarms in office buildings and shut down shipping traffic in the city's harbor. In a number of oceanfront towns, evacuation routes were blocked by wildfires. Thousands were forced to evacuate their homes and wait on beaches for rescue. Thirty-three people died and more than six thousand buildings were destroyed in what was one of the largest wildfires anywhere in the world in the twenty-first century. According to Sydney resident Julie Taylor Mills, "The fires were so big, no one knows how to cope with the enormity of it. . . . We're all scared."[12]

> "The fires were so big, no one knows how to cope with the enormity of it. . . . We're all scared."[12]
>
> —Julie Taylor Mills, resident of New South Wales, Australia

New South Wales is home to some of Australia's most iconic wildlife, including wombats, kangaroos, and kookaburra birds. The impact of the fires on the nation's natural world was devastating. Australian scientists estimated that nearly 3 billion animals were killed, including 143 million mammals, 2.4 billion reptiles, 180 million birds, and 51 million frogs. (Insects were not included in the count.) As Dermot O'Gorman, chief executive officer of World Wide Fund for Nature–Australia, explains, "This ranks as one of the worst wildlife disasters in modern history. It's hard to think of another event anywhere in the world in living memory that has killed or displaced that many animals."[13]

West Coast Wildfires

Climatologists who studied the Australian wildfires confirmed what many already suspected. Climate change is creating high-risk weather conditions that make megafires like Australia's Black Summer much more likely. The delicate balance between temperature, humidity, and rainfall that ruled Australia's natural world for millennia is being thrown off kilter as the climate warms. According to World Weather Attribution, an international climate science institute, human-influenced changes in climate made the heat wave that triggered the Black Summer ten times more likely than it would have been in 1900. And the problems are not confined to Australia, as journalist David Wallace-Wells writes: "California is Australia now."[14]

Wallace-Wells was referring to an unprecedented dry-lightning storm in California in August 2020 that produced nearly fourteen thousand strikes in three days. The lightning ignited fires across a vast swath of the state. Plants and brush were tinder dry due to a string of heat waves and unusually long periods without rain. And winds were so strong that some fires ran through 20 miles (32 km) of terrain in twenty-four hours. There were so many blazes that the state's firefighting agency, Cal Fire, could not keep track of them all—only the 376 largest fires were counted. Twenty-three of the fires, mostly in central and Northern California, were considered major blazes. Several gigantic fires were categorized as complex fires, those that are made up of multiple smaller fires that joined together.

"[The 2020 Australian wildfires rank] as one of the worst wildlife disasters in modern history. It's hard to think of another event anywhere in the world . . . that has killed or displaced that many animals."[13]

—Dermot O'Gorman, chief executive officer of World Wide Fund for Nature–Australia

Wildfires that broke out in Australia in September of 2019 resulted in the death of 3 billion animals, including kangaroos, wombats, and kookaburra birds.

It had been less than two years since 1.67 million acres (675,825 ha) burned in California during what was then a record-setting 2018 wildfire season. The 2020 fires quickly broke those records as nearly 4.2 million acres (1.7 million ha) went up in flames in a matter of weeks. The destruction was so widespread that Cal Fire warned that every citizen of the state—40 million people—should be prepared to evacuate. At least one hundred thousand people did evacuate their homes. Smoke from the fires covered the western United States and two Canadian provinces. On September 9 the smoke blotted out the sun over San Francisco and large areas to the north. The skies took on an eerie, dark orange hue many compared to the atmosphere on Mars. A new term—*gigafires*—was added to the language to describe some of the conflagrations. A gigafire burns at least 1 million acres (404,686 ha) of land, while a megafire burns more than 100,000 acres (40,469 ha).

In 2020 smoke and ash from forest fires in Northern California created a thick orange haze. On September 9, the smoke blotted out the sun over San Francisco.

California was not the only state affected by severe drought and extreme winds. In Oregon more than 1 million acres (404,686 ha) burned in early September. On September 7 an unprecedented 300,000 acres (121,406 ha) in Washington burned in a single day. Around the same time, lighting caused massive wildfires in Colorado, where a record 400,000 acres (161,874 ha) of forests and fields burned in the weeks that followed.

Dead Trees and Drought

As in Australia, climate change set the stage in the American West for bigger and more intense fires. While average global temperatures have increased 1.8°F (1°C) due to climate change, California's average increase is closer to 3°F (1.7°C), according to the US Environmental Protection Agency. Snow is melting earlier in the spring in the mountains, and less rain is falling throughout the state. These conditions were blamed for the worst drought in California history, which lasted from 2010 to 2017. The crippling drought weakened the pine trees that covered large swaths of

California mountainsides. This made the trees susceptible to attack by mountain pine beetles, wood borers, and other species of bark beetle. According to the US Forest Service, beetle infestations combined with drought to kill more than 142 million trees in California by 2018. As fire scientist Scott Stephens wrote at the time, "The scale of present tree mortality is so large that greater potential for 'mass fire' exists in the coming decades, driven by the amount . . . of dry, combustible, large woody material that could produce large, severe fires."[15]

Stephens's predictions proved accurate in 2020 when the California gigafires broke out. According to the US Forest Service, around 85 percent of the trees burning in the massive Creek Fire around Shaver Lake in Fresno County were beetle-killed timber. The Creek Fire, which scorched 380,002 acres (153,781 ha) and consumed around nine hundred buildings, was the largest single fire in California history.

With dead pines adding fuel to the flames in California, the world's largest trees are under threat from bigger, hotter fires. Giant sequoias grow in only one place on earth—the western

Bark Beetles Thrive in Warmer, Drier Climate

Bark beetles were once considered beneficial insects in North America's forests. They allowed young pines to gain a foothold on the forest floor by attacking weak, dying trees. Beetle numbers were kept in check by cold winters, but climate change has altered this balance. Winters have grown milder; summers have gotten hotter and drier. These changes have allowed the bark beetle population to thrive and, in the process, cut a swath of destruction through mountain forests. Healthy trees can resist wildfires, but trees killed by beetles provide fuel that turns low-intensity fires into megafires or gigafires.

Bark beetles, which are no bigger than a grain of rice, have destroyed millions of pine trees in the western United States and Canada. Around six hundred species of bark beetle exist in North America, but one species is especially destructive. The mountain pine beetle has killed about 100,000 square miles (258,999 sq. km) of trees in North America since 2000. The beetles are considered the most damaging insect blight ever seen, and no one has found a way to stop them.

slopes of California's Sierra Nevada mountain range. The tallest sequoias reach a height of 310 feet (94 m)—the size of a thirty-story building—and they might be as thick as 35 feet (10.7 m) at the base. Giant sequoias can live more than three thousand years, and the oldest trees are referred to as monarchs. Like the eucalyptus trees in Australia, giant sequoias evolved over millennia to withstand wildfires. Sequoias are protected from flames by bark that is up to 3 feet (91.4 cm) thick. The branches and needles of the trees are high above the forest floor, so flames from typical wildfires cannot reach them. The seeds of sequoia trees are packed into small cones that are coated with a waxy substance. The cones can survive up to twenty years until a forest fire melts the wax. The seeds are released and fertilized by minerals in the burned soil.

California's sequoia groves have survived countless wildfires and droughts. And the trees can survive if only 5 percent of their green needles do not burn in a fire. But in recent years a new kind of hotter wildfire has been burning through the sequoia groves. In 2020 the Sequoia Complex fire, ignited by lightning, burned around 171,000 acres (69,200 ha), reducing thousands of sequoia trees to cinders. Christy Brigham, science chief of Sequoia and Kings Canyon National Parks, says she was not worried about the fire at first: "I still had the mental model that these trees are very fire-adapted. . . . This is going to be OK from the sequoia perspective." But after the flames were extinguished, Brigham saw numerous sequoias whose crowns were completely incinerated. "To see those giant sequoia [turned into] blackened toothpicks was a gut punch,"[16] Brigham says. Several factors contributed to the destruction. The sequoia groves, like many forests in the West, are overgrown with brush and small pines. This underbrush acts like a ladder that allows flames to climb up into

> "To see those giant sequoia [turned into] blackened toothpicks was a gut punch."[16]
>
> —Christy Brigham, Sequoia and Kings Canyon National Parks science chief

the crowns of mature trees. In past centuries Native Americans set small, controlled fires to clear out the underbrush. The US Forest Service, which manages much of the wildlands in the West, lacks funds to thin the underbrush and remove smaller trees.

Weather Created by Wildfires

When forests burn on a large scale, the destruction goes beyond incinerated trees. Burning forests also accelerate climate change. The fires release massive amounts of CO_2, which further warms the world, producing weather conditions that will lead to more combustible forests. And some wildfires are so immense that they cause their own freakish weather systems in real time. These systems, called firestorms, can create fire lightning and fire tornadoes.

Firestorms are caused when the immense heat produced by a blaze draws in vast quantities of oxygen. This creates a powerful updraft of rapidly moving air that funnels smoke, ash, and burning particles into the atmosphere like a smokestack. The air cools

Some wildfires are so immense that they cause firestorms that create phenomena such as fire tornados.

quickly in the upper atmosphere, causing it to condense into droplets of water. These droplets form massive grayish-brown fire clouds called pyrocumulus clouds.

If the firestorm continues to grow, the updraft funnels even more smoke and debris into the sky. This allows the formation of even bigger clouds called pyrocumulonimbus clouds, abbreviated as pyroCbs. These ominous clouds look like mud-colored thunderclouds but are far more dangerous. Rather than moving across the land as thunderclouds do, pyroCbs remain in place, tethered to the massive fire that created them. PyroCbs hurl powerful lightning bolts down to earth, prompting NASA to refer to them as the "fire-breathing dragon of clouds."[17] Fire lightning, combined with spewing embers and intense, hot winds, further fuels the wildfire, making it grow even larger.

On rare occasions pyroCbs can trigger fire tornadoes, perhaps one of the most frighting weather phenomena on earth. Fire

What Tree Rings Say About Drought

Scientists long ago identified the damaging effects of prolonged drought on people and wildlife. What they have not been able to do until recently is understand the connection between climate change and drought. That changed in 2019 when Columbia University researchers used tree-ring records to look back in time to study climate history. What those tree rings told them is that human activities began influencing global drought as far back as 1900.

Trees grow more during rainy years, which produces thicker rings in trees. During periods of drought trees grow less, which is revealed by thinner rings. When researchers analyzed tree rings dating back six hundred to nine hundred years they found natural variations between wet years and dry years. These fluctuations were compared to tree-ring growth since the early twentieth century when fossil fuel consumption rapidly grew. Tree rings indicated that the number of drought years increased dramatically in North America, Europe, Australia, and elsewhere due to coal-powered industrial production and the invention of the gas-fueled automobile. As Kate Marvel, lead scientist on the Columbia study, explained: "It really did surprise me, personally—the thought that humans could have influenced global drought that far back in time is really stunning."

Quoted in Daisy Dunne, "Climate Change Has Influenced Global Drought Risk for 'More than a Century,'" Carbon Brief, May 1, 2019. www.carbonbrief.org.

tornadoes form when the air over a wildfire rises very quickly and forms a blazing funnel cloud. Some reach tornado-like speeds of 140 miles per hour (225 kph) but are searing hot, up to 2,700°F (1,482°C). Fire tornadoes were observed in the Carr Fire, which burned almost 230,000 acres (93,078 ha) and killed at least seven people in California in July 2018. The pyroCb cloud that formed the tornadoes grew in size from nearly 4 miles (6.4 km) to more than 7 miles (11.3 km) in just fifteen minutes. The fire tornadoes spawned by the cloud traveled up to three-quarters of a mile (1.2 km), setting fire to everything they touched. And this was not the biggest fire tornado ever seen. One that formed during a fire in Canberra, Australia, in 2003 traveled 12 miles (19.3 km) before collapsing on itself.

Fire tornadoes are very unusual; pyroCbs more commonly generate fire whirls, which are smaller and slower. Fire whirls only travel a few hundred feet before falling apart. However, scientists say the conditions that fueled the fire tornado during the Carr Fire will become more common as wildfires continue to grow in size.

Breaking Records

By the end of 2020, over 5 million acres (2 million ha) had burned in California, Oregon, and Washington. According to climate scientist Daniel Swain, "We've broken almost every record there is to break."[18] And records are being broken in forested regions around the globe. Massive fires have consumed vast swaths of the Amazon rain forest, southern Africa, Indonesia, and Siberia. And the records are bound to fall as the climate continues to warm.

Few disasters better illustrate the problem of a planet rapidly heating, as David Wallace-Wells states: "Fires are among the best and more horrifying [publicists] for climate change. . . . They offer up vivid, scarring images [that are] portents of future nightmares even as they document present tragedies and horrors."[19]

CHAPTER 3

Record Rainstorms and Flooding

Locusts are plant-eating insects that have long been seen as a curse to humanity. Locust swarms were described in ancient Egypt, Greece, and China. In the Bible (Exodus 10:4–5), God threatens to punish the Egyptians with a plague of locusts: "I will bring locusts into your country tomorrow. They will cover the face of the ground so that it cannot be seen. They will devour what little you have left . . . including every tree that is growing in your fields. They will fill your houses and those of all your officials and all the Egyptians."[20]

In 2020 people in East Africa experienced a locust plague of biblical proportions. The insects devoured wheat and sorghum crops, fruit and nut tree orchards, and plants growing in the wild. Swarms of locusts destroyed food supplies that tens of millions of people depend on in Kenya, Ethiopia, Uganda, Somalia, and elsewhere. Locust were also swarming in Pakistan, India, and Saudi Arabia. According to the Food and Agriculture Organization of the United Nations, the locust swarms posed a threat to the livelihoods of 10 percent of the world's population. As science reporter Madeleine Stone describes it, "City-sized swarms of the dreaded pests are wreaking havoc as they descend on crops and pasturelands, devouring everything in a matter of hours. The scale of the locust outbreak . . . is like nothing in recent memory."[21]

The plague of voracious locusts was caused by exceptionally wet weather in places that traditionally see very little rain. The insects, referred to as desert locusts, resemble harmless grasshoppers under normal weather conditions. But when heavy rainfalls occur in deserts, the insects rapidly multiply and grow much larger than usual. The insects' behavior also changes, according to insect scientist Rick Overson: "They become attracted to one another—and if those [wet] conditions persist in the environment, they start to [fly] together in coordinated formations across the landscape, which is what we're seeing in eastern Africa."[22] Scientists are unsure why locusts transform in this way, but when they do, it is devastating. An average of 60 million locusts can pack into half a square mile (1.3 sq. km). In just one day, a swarm that size can devour an amount of food that would normally feed twenty-five hundred people. And the 2020 swarms were much larger; in Kenya a massive cloud of locusts measured 25 miles (40.2 km) long by 37 miles (59.5 km) wide. These locusts moved across the landscape at speeds reaching more than 60 miles (97 km) per day.

"City-sized swarms of [locusts] are wreaking havoc as they descend on crops and pasturelands, devouring everything in a matter of hours."[21]

—Madeleine Stone, science reporter

Scientists blame the plague of locusts on two freak storms in 2018. Heavy rain fell on the deserts of southern Saudi Arabia and northern Yemen. The rain allowed the locusts to reproduce as they spread into Iran, Somalia, and Ethiopia. Unusually wet autumn rains in 2019 kept conditions favorable for the insects. By early 2020 the locusts were breeding in large numbers and creating havoc in East Africa, where the abnormally wet weather conditions persisted.

Researchers studying the locust outbreak have blamed climate change for the unusually large number of heavy downpours in the Arabian Desert. Basic science is behind this trend. More than 70 percent of the planet is water, and as the climate warms, more moisture from the oceans evaporates into the atmosphere. When it rains, there is more water volume in the clouds, creating stronger downpours. The intense rain in the Arabian Desert was

Unusually wet weather can cause population explosions among destructive insects such as locusts. In 2020 locust swarms posed a threat to the livelihoods of 10 percent of the world's population.

caused by storms that formed over the Indian Ocean, which was nearly 4°F (2.2°C) warmer than average. Moisture evaporating from the warm ocean waters increased rainfall amounts by more than 400 percent above normal in the region, according to the United Nations Environment Programme. And United Nations climate scientist Richard Munang says Africa can expect more locust plagues in the future: "Studies have linked a hotter climate to more damaging locust swarms, leaving Africa disproportionately affected—20 of the fastest warming countries globally are in Africa."[23]

The Great Flood of 2019

Rising temperatures and more moisture in the air are combining to cause problems in the midwestern United States, where the average number of heavy rainfalls has doubled over the past century. And according to a February 2019 study by scientists at the University of Notre Dame, extreme rainstorms in states such as in Indiana, Iowa, Kansas, Missouri, Nebraska, and Wisconsin are expected to increase by 30 percent by the end of this century. If predictions are correct this spike in precipitation will impact the nation's ability to produce food.

The US Department of Agriculture says midwestern states produce an estimated $76 billion in crops and livestock products annually. With 127 million acres (51.4 million ha) of agricultural land, the Midwest farm belt supplies 25 percent of the world's grain crops, including soy, corn, wheat, and rice. This region also produces carrots, cabbage, grapes, onions, strawberries, and many more foods found on grocers' shelves.

Farmers depend on rainfall to water their crops, but too much rain can be destructive. This was the case in March 2019, when record rainstorms and floods swamped farms across the Midwest. Nearly 35 inches (89 cm) of precipitation, in the form of rain and snow, fell across the region, around 5 inches (12.7 cm)

Mexico's Freak Hailstorm

Hail is produced within thunderstorms when warm, moist air from the ground is pulled high into the stratosphere. Even in summer months, temperatures at this level can be cold enough to freeze the water into balls of ice. As hailstones grow in size, they get too heavy to remain aloft, so they fall to the ground. While summer hailstorms are not unusual, the one that hit Guadalajara, Mexico, in June 2019 was bizarre by any measure. Temperatures were around 88°F (31°C) when a slow-moving thunderstorm dumped more than 3 feet (91.4 cm) of marble-sized hailstones on the city. The rain that accompanied the hail caused flash floods that turned Guadalajara streets into fast-moving rivers of icy slush that swept away cars and trucks. Hundreds of homes and businesses were damaged. After the storm the state governor, Enrique Alfaro, tweeted, "I've never seen such scenes. Then we ask ourselves if climate change is real."

Scientists say a single storm, even of this magnitude, cannot be traced directly to climate change. But climate change is contributing to conditions that make powerful hailstorms more likely. As the climate warms, it pulls more moisture into the atmosphere, which creates conditions like those that led to the Guadalajara hailstorm.

Quoted in Michael Le Page, "Was Mexico's Freak Summer Hail Storm Due to Global Warming?," *New Scientist*, July 1, 2019. www.newscientist.com.

above average. Five extra inches of precipitation might not sound like much. But the wet weather was blamed for the historically destructive flooding across fifteen states in the central part of the country, affecting the lives of 14 million people.

The extreme weather began in mid-March, when midwestern temperatures quickly rose to 60°F (15.6°C) after an unusually snowy winter that left several feet of snow on the ground. The snowpack could not absorb the rain, which washed directly into streams and rivers. This led to what is now called the Great Flood of 2019 as ice, snowmelt, and rain flooded hundreds of miles of land along the Arkansas, Mississippi, and Missouri Rivers. Floodwaters breached levees, damaged thousands of homes, and washed away roads, bridges, and railroads farmers depend on to bring their crops to market.

The storms were accompanied by extremely high winds. Nebraska experienced a freakish weather phenomenon called a bomb cyclone. Extremely low atmospheric pressure, very high winds, and drenching rains are the main features of a bomb cyclone. The low pressure forces a massive column of air from the ground into the atmosphere, leaving a void. Surrounding air rushes into this void, creating winds that can range from 80 to 100 miles per hour (129 to 161 kph). The Nebraska bomb cyclone caused the most extensive damage in state history, costing an estimated $1.3 billion. Bryan Tuma, assistant director of Nebraska's Emergency Management Agency, commented on the scope of the damages: "I would describe it as biblical."[24]

Bomb cyclones are normally rare; one hits the United States an average of once a year. But like other extreme weather events, the number of bomb cyclones is growing. According to Michael Mann, director of the Penn State Earth System Science Center, climate change is increasing "the development of more intense bomb cyclones . . . packing tropical storm–scale winds and dumping huge amounts of precipitation."[25] There were at least four bomb cyclones in 2019, including one in November in Oregon that was described as unprecedented by the National

Rapidly rising temperatures in the spring of 2019 caused massive flooding in the Midwest. This bridge in Nebraska was washed away by rushing water.

Weather Service. This bomb cyclone was remarkable for producing the lowest air pressure ever observed on earth at sea level, a phenomenon that produced hurricane-force winds with gusts measured at 106 miles per hour (171 kph) in Cape Blanco on Oregon's Pacific coast.

More Moisture, More Destruction

The extreme storms of 2019 continued into July, when the jet stream was blamed for destructive weather in eastern parts of the United States. Instead of following its normal summer flow from west to east, the jet stream coiled into a north-south pattern more typical of early spring. This created a low-pressure system that stalled a storm over Washington, DC, that dropped 4 inches (10 cm) of rain in a single hour. Roads quickly flooded, stranding hundreds of motorists in their vehicles. Local streams and rivers rose more than 10 feet (3 m) in a few hours, causing flash floods across the region. At least a dozen people were rescued from the rising waters.

According to the National Weather Service, storms of this magnitude are exceedingly rare; odds of a rainstorm with this intensity are less than 1 percent in any given year. Despite the long odds, a similar storm hit nearby Baltimore exactly one month later, unleashing a month's worth of rain—6 inches (15.2 cm)—in a two-hour period. The Baltimore storm also brought 70-mile-per-hour (113 kph) winds and hail the size of Ping-Pong balls, which dented cars, damaged roofs, and broke tree branches. The National Weather Service once again said such storms were very unusual; the odds of that amount of rain falling in such a short period are one in one thousand in an average year. However, according to the 2018 National Climate Assessment, "The frequency and intensity of heavy precipitation events across the United States have increased . . . and are expected to continue to increase over the coming century."[26]

The intense storms of 2019 continued into September, when four times the normal amount of rain fell in Montana, North and South Dakota, and Nebraska. The rains disrupted the lives of farmers who depend on dry autumn weather to harvest their crops. And some towns had not yet repaired the damages to levees, roads, and bridges from the previous spring's rains. The storms produced a record amount of water flowing into the Missouri River, which caused interstate highways to close while triggering flood warnings and evacuations in Omaha, Nebraska, and elsewhere.

Unpredictable Weather

The rainstorms of 2019 caused over $15 billion in damages, and some of the areas that flooded were not expected to recover for years. The extreme rains were not confined to the United States that year. In November in northern England, some areas experienced a month's worth of average rainfall in a single day. Firefighters had to rescue more than forty people trapped by rising waters in the town of Doncaster. Residents said it was the first time the village had flooded in more than a century.

East Africa experienced flooding and landslides during October and through December 2019, which affected the lives of 2.8 million people. Some areas received more than double the average rainfall amounts. In India the yearly monsoon rains, which

In 2019 torrential monsoon rains caused floods in India that killed at least thirteen hundred people and displaced millions.

last from July to September, were the heaviest in at least twenty-five years. The record torrential rainfalls that began in July killed at least thirteen hundred people and displaced millions. Farmers in India depend on the annual monsoons, but the rains can be a mixed blessing, as reporter Vaishnavi Chandrashekhar explains:

> For centuries, Indians have rejoiced at the arrival of the monsoon to break summer's fever. . . . Increasingly, however, the season's sweet relief is laced with apprehension. The torrential rains that submerged parts of India this year are . . . caused by record rainfall—a scenario that many worry could become the "new normal" as climate change increases the frequency of extreme weather.[27]

With extreme weather as the new normal from India to East Africa to the midwestern United States, the natural cycles food producers depend on are becoming less predictable. Farmers rarely have perfect weather, but climate change is adding an extra level of uncertainty to the business of agriculture. In Iowa, Nebraska, and South Dakota, some areas that were inundated with rain in 2019 were drought stricken in 2020. Illinois State Farm Bureau director Earl Williams put the 2020 weather extremes in perspective: "We like to say it's always 'too hot, too cold, too wet, too dry' because we always complain about things we can't control. But this is not a typical year because it was 'too hot, too cold, too wet, too dry' all in one year."[28] While locusts have not yet invaded the Midwest, changing weather patterns are affecting the lives of millions of people who expect the rains to be dependable and productive rather than dangerous and destructive.

"This is not a typical year because it was 'too hot, too cold, too wet, too dry' all in one year."[28]

—Earl Williams, director of Illinois State Farm Bureau

CHAPTER 4

Monster Hurricanes

The Atlantic Ocean is a powerful weather maker in Central America, the Caribbean, and the southeastern United States. Every year from June through November, the ocean produces numerous tropical storms with sustained winds of 39 to 73 miles per hour (63 to 117 kph). The Atlantic also whips up hurricanes, with winds above 74 miles per hour (119 kph). Historically, there have been so many storms in the region that the National Weather Service decided it needed a better way to keep track of them. In 1953 the bureau began giving female names, in alphabetical order, to tropical storms and hurricanes in the Atlantic. That year the fourteen storms ranged from Alice to Irene. In 1979 men's names were added to the list.

In 2020 the task of naming storms grew more difficult; the hurricane season saw a record number of storms in the shortest amount of time in history. By September weather forecasters had run through the entire English-language alphabet, so they began naming hurricanes after letters from the Greek alphabet. On November 17, 2020, Hurricane Iota hit Nicaragua with 30 inches (76 cm) of rain, catastrophic winds of 120 to 140 miles per hour (193 to 225 kph), and flooding that threatened tens of thousands of people. Iota was the record-breaking thirtieth named storm of the season, but it was unusual for another reason: It was the second major hurricane to hit Puerto Cabezas, Nicaragua, within a two-week period. According to meteorologist Matthew Cappucci, hurricanes have never before hit the same place twice in such a short period of time: "It's virtually unprecedented. We combed through the books and turned up nothing like this before. . . . Having two Category 4 hurricanes strike within 15 miles in just two weeks is something we couldn't find matched in nearly 170 years of data. It's yet another staggering record to fall in the 2020 hurricane season."[29]

As Cappucci notes, Hurricane Iota was a Category 4 storm. That means it had sustained winds of 130 to 156 miles per hour (209 to 251 kph)—strong enough to cause catastrophic damage. Forecasters classify hurricanes on what is called the Saffir-Simpson Hurricane Wind Scale—a 1 to 5 rating that is based on maximum sustained wind speed. According to the National Hurricane Center, Category 1 storms have winds of 74 to 95 miles per hour (119 to 153 kph). Category 5 hurricanes are the most destructive, with sustained winds of over 157 miles per hour (253 kph). Any hurricane, regardless of category, can be lethal. There were three Category 1 hurricanes in 2020. One of them, Hurricane Isaias, killed one in Puerto Rico, two in the Dominican Republic, and sixteen in the United States.

> "Having two Category 4 hurricanes strike within 15 miles in just two weeks is something we couldn't find matched in nearly 170 years of data."[29]
>
> —Matthew Cappucci, meteorologist

Hot Water, Stronger Hurricanes

According to NASA, the most powerful hurricanes can expend as much energy during their life cycle as ten thousand nuclear bombs. That destructive force is increasing as climate change alters hurricane behavior. Hurricanes typically occur where ocean waters are at least 80°F (27°C) down to a depth of 150 feet (47.5 m). The most powerful hurricanes form in water that is even warmer. As climate change heats up the world's oceans, the likelihood of more high-intensity hurricanes has grown. Since 1970 the oceans have absorbed 90 percent of the excess heat generated by the buildup of CO_2 and other globe-warming gases in the atmosphere. This has heated ocean surface temperatures by an average of 1°F (0.56°C) over the past century. As environmental journalist Alejandra Borunda explains, "Warm water acts as [a] storehouse of energy that storms can draw on, like a battery: the hotter the water, or the more of it there is, the more energy can be transferred into the air above."[30]

Warm air holds more moisture than cold air. So when unusually high air temperatures combine with higher-than-normal ocean temperatures, as has happened in many hurricane-prone areas of the world, the

> "Warm water acts as [a] storehouse of energy that storms can draw on, like a battery: the hotter the water . . . the more energy can be transferred into the air above."[30]
>
> —Alejandra Borunda, environmental journalist

Record Rainfall

With climate change producing wetter hurricanes, new records for precipitation are being set nearly every year. In August 2017 Hurricane Harvey hit Texas with winds reaching 130 miles per hour (209 kph). The winds weakened quickly when Harvey made landfall, but the hurricane stalled over Texas for four days. The storm, which was the wettest ever recorded in the United States, dumped a record-setting 60 inches (152 cm) of rain near Port Arthur. The rainfall caused catastrophic flooding in Houston, where nearly 10 inches (25 cm) of rain fell in ninety minutes in some places. The storm left around 30 percent of all land in Harris County, where Houston is located, underwater. Climatologist Andrea Prein explains how Harvey produced this epic rainfall: "Think about an ocean as an infinite supply of moisture. Harvey is sucking it toward land and dumping it on Texas."

As the most significant rainfall event ever to hit the United States, Harvey killed 103 people in storm-related incidents and caused $128 billion in damages. Flooding from the storm damaged or destroyed approximately three hundred thousand structures, along with half a million vehicles. Forty-thousand people were left homeless by the storm. Four scientific studies published after the storm found that human-caused global warming made Harvey's heavy rains more likely.

Quoted in Craig Welch, "How Climate Change Likely Strengthened Recent Hurricanes," National Geographic, September 20, 2017. www.nationalgeographic.com.

result is more rain. According to the NOAA, a rise in both air and water temperatures in these regions has increased the likelihood of smaller hurricanes developing into more dangerous hurricanes by about 32 percent.

Stronger Storm Surges

Warm oceans create more dangerous hurricanes in another way. Warm water takes up more space than cold water, so as the oceans warm, they expand. This process, known as thermal expansion, is causing sea levels to rise. Oceans are also rising as global warming melts ice at the North and South Poles, Greenland, and elsewhere. The combination of thermal expansion and meltwater has caused average global sea levels to rise around 9 inches (23 cm) since 1880. And the process is speeding up; one-third of the rise in sea levels has occurred since 1995.

When high winds push ocean waters onshore during a hurricane, it creates what is called a storm surge. These floodwaters are the greatest threat to life and property from a hurricane, and rising ocean levels are creating bigger and more dangerous storm surges. The destructive force of higher seas combined with surging ocean water made headlines in 2012 when Hurricane Sandy

High seas and surging ocean waters that accompanied Hurricane Sandy in 2012 destroyed homes, boardwalks, and roadways in coastal areas of New York State and the surrounding region.

hit the East Coast of the United States. In New York City the storm surge from the Category 3 storm flooded subway tunnels, roads, parks, and other infrastructure, causing billions of dollars in damages. In nearby areas, Sandy's surge destroyed homes, boardwalks, roadways, and an amusement park.

> "Sea level rise means we'll see [a] . . . greater frequency of coastal flooding from storms, even if storms don't get any stronger."[31]
>
> —Cynthia Rosenzweig, NASA climate scientist

Scientists say New York Harbor has experienced a 12-inch (30.5 cm) rise in sea level over the past century. And according to NASA climate scientist Cynthia Rosenzweig, "For Sandy, that meant greater coastal flooding in New York and the surrounding region than we would have experienced a century ago. Continuing to climb the staircase of sea level rise means we'll see greater extent and greater frequency of coastal flooding from storms, even if storms don't get any stronger."[31]

Slow Moving and Deadly

Hot air temperatures combined with a storm surge to produce one of the most devastating hurricanes ever to hit the United States. In October 2018 extremely warm ocean temperatures created what is referred to as a marine heat wave. This heat wave brought water temperatures in the Gulf of Mexico to a very hot 90°F (32°C). Around this time Hurricane Michael was barreling through the Caribbean toward Florida, leaving a path of destruction in its wake. The hurricane gathered strength from the hot water, becoming a monster Category 5 hurricane, the first to make landfall in the United States since 1992. Michael hit the Florida Panhandle with peak winds of 160 miles per hour (257 kph). The storm dumped around 10 inches (25 cm) of rain on Florida. When combined with the storm surge, Hurricane Michael submerged normally dry areas around Port St. Joe under 9 to 14 feet (2.7 to 4.3 m) of water. The storm, which caused around $25 billion in damages, was blamed for the deaths of fifty-nine people in the United States and fifteen in Central America.

Hurricane Michael came less than a month after the Category 4 Hurricane Florence battered North and South Carolina with record-setting catastrophic rains totaling 30 inches (76 cm) in some places. A study of Florence by climate scientists at the Lawrence Berkeley National Laboratory in California showed that rainfall from the storm was 50 percent worse than it would have been without climate change. The hurricane's spectacular size, around 50 miles (80 km) across, was also blamed on the warmer oceans and atmospheric temperatures caused by climate change.

Florence was weird in a different way. The storm moved much slower than the average hurricane, which typically travels across ocean waters at around 350 miles (563 km) per day. When a fast-moving hurricane makes landfall, it no longer gains energy from the ocean; the winds die down, and the storm dumps rain

Scientists blame climate change for the unusually slow movement of Hurricane Florence—shown here in a satellite photo—which dumped catastrophic rains on North and South Carolina.

over a wide area as it moves across the land. Florence slowed to a relative crawl, covering only 80 miles (129 km) a day as it approached the Carolinas. When Florence made landfall it nearly stopped. Part of the hurricane remained over the ocean sucking up moisture while the leading edge stalled over land, dropping a hurricane's worth of drenching rains for several days over a small area of the coast.

Scientists blame climate change for slower-moving hurricanes like Florence. While the exact cause is unknown, a 2018 study by the science journal *Nature* showed that hurricanes in the United States have slowed by 16 percent since 1949. As atmospheric research scientist James Kossin explains:

> Storms can get worse without getting more intense [if they are slow moving]. . . . That's just through very fundamental mathematics, because if you slow down how fast a storm is moving through a neighborhood, there's probably more rain; storm surge would probably be greater; and while wind speeds won't get any stronger, the amount of time that structures are hit by that wind would get longer.[32]

The Strongest Storm on Earth

While the storms that rage in the Atlantic are called hurricanes, the exact same weather phenomenon is called a typhoon in the northwestern Pacific Ocean. The term *super typhoons* is used to describe storms equal to Category 4 or 5 hurricanes. In the South Pacific and Indian Oceans, hurricanes are called cyclones. Whatever they are called, these storms, like Atlantic hurricanes, are becoming more extreme due to warmer temperatures in the ocean and in the atmosphere.

In late October 2020 the massive Super Typhoon Goni made landfall in the Philippines. Goni was especially strong because the Pacific Ocean was extremely warm in 2020. Goni started as a typical typhoon near Guam but gathered strength as it passed

Extremely hot weather caused by climate change is having an effect on ocean surface temperatures. This is making seawater in some places hotter than it ever was before. A prolonged period of above-average ocean water temperatures is known as a marine heat wave. These heat waves can persist for weeks, months, or even years. Marine heat waves have harmed ocean ecosystems and are also blamed for causing hurricanes to grow larger, wetter, and more destructive than in the past.

According to a study by the journal *Nature*, the number of days with abnormally high temperatures in upper ocean levels increased 82 percent from 1982 to 2018. In 2020 the entire East Coast of the United States, from Florida to Maine, experienced record high ocean temperatures due to a massive marine heat wave. This was blamed for fueling the most active hurricane season on record. As climatologist Malin Pinsky explains, "[Research] makes clear that heatwaves are hitting the ocean all over the world. . . . The ocean, in effect, is spiking a fever. . . . These events are likely to become more extreme and more common in the future unless we can reduce greenhouse gas emissions."

Quoted in Damian Carrington, "Heatwaves Sweeping Oceans 'Like Wildfires,' Scientists Reveal," *The Guardian* (Manchester, UK), March 4, 2019. www.theguardian.com.

over waters that were around 87°F (31°C)—or 3°F (1.7°C) warmer than normal. Infrared satellite images of the storm taken by weather satellites show Goni transforming from a disorganized pattern of clouds into a circling Category 5 storm with winds of 180 miles per hour (290 kph). As seen in NASA satellite images, the storm resembled a whirling buzzsaw.

By the time Goni hit the Philippine island of Catanduanes on November 1, peak winds had increased to 195 miles per hour (314 kph). These violent winds put Goni in the NOAA record books as the strongest tropical cyclone ever to make landfall. The typhoon left a trail of destruction on the small island, destroying buildings and roads, toppling trees, and causing massive mudslides. At least ten people were killed in the floodwaters caused by the torrential rain and 15-foot (4.6 m) storm surge. There was some good news, however. The typhoon collapsed rapidly after making landfall, sparing the densely populated Philippine capital city, Manila.

While Goni was the most powerful storm in world history, it was only slightly stronger than other typhoons that have hit the Philippines in recent years. Super Typhoon Haiyan (2013) and Super Typhoon Meranti (2016) had slightly slower winds of 190 miles per hour (306 kph) when making landfall.

A detailed 2018 study of tropical storms by researchers at Princeton University predicted that ultra-powerful typhoons with winds over 190 miles per hour (306 kph) will become more common. In the twentieth century storms of this strength averaged once every eight years. By the end of the twenty-first century, scientists have warned, these mega typhoons could be an annual occurrence. As climate scientist Jeff Masters writes, these predictions, while dire, were conditioned on nations taking solid

In October of 2020 the Super Typhoon Goni hit the Philippines, resulting in flooding and massive mudslides that killed at least ten people.

steps to slow climate change. This is not happening, as Masters explains: "Under the 'business-as-usual' track we are currently on, the [Princeton University study] might have predicted an even greater increase in ultra-intense tropical cyclones. The fact that we've seen four megastorms [nearly] as strong as . . . Goni over the past eight years is a troubling sign."[33]

An Uncontrolled Experiment

According to the NOAA, the world's oceans are warming at a quickening pace, about 24 percent faster than they did in the 1990s. And this is affecting storms in another way. As warmer water covers more of the earth, the range of tropical hurricanes is expanding. Storms are predicted to occur in cooler regions, where people are not prepared to deal with high winds and drenching rains. For example, powerful hurricanes have never hit Southern California, where the average ocean temperature in the summer is around 70°F (21°C). But in August 2020, as a heat wave baked the region, the Pacific Ocean hit a record 79.5°F (26.4°C) off the San Diego coast. Technically, that water temperature is warm enough for hurricanes to form. This means that people in Southern California might one day be exposed to the kind of winds, rains, and storm surges that are a reality in Florida, the Caribbean, and elsewhere.

Hurricanes and other weather patterns are a product of sun-warmed air, cloud-forming water vapor, and the vast ocean waters. These forces exchange massive amounts of energy to produce winds and rain. While hurricanes have always been destructive and deadly, they were limited by natural atmospheric forces. Humanity has upset this equation by building a world reliant on fossil fuels. This has created what might be referred to as an uncontrolled experiment, with civilization emitting millions of tons of climate-warming gases into the oceans and the atmosphere every year. The outcome of this experiment remains uncertain as the number of hot spells and marine heat waves grows with each passing year.

CHAPTER 5

Deadly Cold and Snow

Chicago can be a very cold place to live. During any given winter, Chicagoans might experience snow, bitter winds, and subfreezing temperatures. But even by Chicago standards, the winter of 2019 was extremely cold. On January 30 Chicago logged a record-breaking high temperature of -10°F (-23°C). In the hours that followed, thermometers bottomed out at -23°F (-31°C). The frigid temperatures were coupled with strong winds, creating a life-threatening windchill that made the temperature feel like -52°F (-47°C). The next night air temperatures in nearby Rockville, Illinois, plunged to a record low -31°F (-35°C). The below-zero cold snap occurred days after Chicago came close to setting snowfall records. Snow fell every day from January 17 to 29, accumulating nearly 15 inches (38 cm). Some of these snowfalls were classified as blizzards: winter storms with heavy snow and strong winds that create whiteout conditions where visibility is reduced to zero.

The Siberia-like weather prompted Chicago residents to nickname their city "Chiberia" as schools and businesses closed and daily life ground to a halt. Chicago is located on Lake Michigan. According to local meteorologist Tom Skilling, the lake "took on the appearance of a boiling cauldron as air of minus 20 degrees and colder made contact with water sitting just above the freezing level. I've lived here 40 years and never until today have [I] seen a more spectacular display of 'sea smoke.'"[34]

Videos appeared on social media of people blowing soap bubbles that froze in midair and crashed to the ground. Others tossed boiling water out of saucepans, watching as it turned into snow-like ice before it hit the ground. However, for many the cold was deadly serious. At those icy windchill temperatures, exposed skin can freeze within minutes, causing painful frostbite. Across the Midwest at least twenty-two people died from the cold.

"[Lake Michigan] took on the appearance of a boiling cauldron as air of minus 20 degrees and colder made contact with water sitting just above the freezing level."[34]

—Tom Skilling, meteorologist

Blame the Polar Vortex

Chicago's deep freeze was caused by a concentration of Arctic air known as the polar vortex. The vortex is a pool of extremely cold air that normally sits over the North Pole. This swirling mass of very cold Arctic air constantly rotates counterclockwise, west to east, over the top of the earth. The polar vortex is normally a single current of cold air that remains in the north. When the vortex weakens, it breaks into two or more smaller sections. When this happens, the polar vortex sends frigid air south, bringing colder-than-normal temperatures to the northern United States, Canada, Europe, and elsewhere. As meteorologist Matthew Cappucci explains, "Most of the time, [the polar vortex's] harsh conditions are out of reach. But every so often, lobes of it pinch off from the main flow and crash south. This can lash the Lower 48 [states] with piercing shots of cold, intense bouts of storminess and bitter wind chills well below zero."[35]

"[The polar vortex] can lash the Lower 48 [states] with piercing shots of cold, intense bouts of storminess and bitter wind chills well below zero."[35]

—Matthew Cappucci, meteorologist

The polar vortex that brought piercing cold to Chicago stalled over the central part of the country. Record low temperatures created problems in Indiana, Kentucky, Michigan, Minnesota, Ohio, and elsewhere. In Iowa, records fell when thermometers hit -30°F (-34°C) with dangerously low -58°F (-50°C) windchills. The Des Moines office of the National Weather Service issued a warning: "This is the coldest air many of us will have ever experienced. This is not a case of 'meh, it's Iowa during winter and this cold happens.' These are record-breaking cold air temperatures, with wind chill values not seen in the 21st century in Iowa."[36]

In March 2019 weird winter weather continued to impact North America. A system the Weather Channel named Winter Storm Ulmer brought cold, snow, and ice to large portions of the United States. Ulmer was one of the strongest winter storms on record, producing blizzards with extremely high winds. The storm originated in Colorado, where heavy snow was accompanied by winds of up to 110 miles per hour (177 kph). The storm swept northeast,

A weather phenomenon known as a polar vortex in the winter of 2019 caused temperatures in Chicago to plunge so low that residents nicknamed their city "Chiberia."

creating blizzard-like conditions in the Dakotas, Wyoming, and elsewhere. Ulmer was memorable for another reason. It produced a bomb cyclone in Colorado, where records for the lowest atmospheric pressure were smashed. The winter bomb cyclone brought blizzards and hurricane-force winds to northeast Colorado for more than ten hours. Colorado Springs measured the highest gust from the bomb cyclone, 96 miles per hour (154 kph). This smashed the previous all-time record wind speed in Colorado Springs, which was 80 miles per hour (129 kph). Trees and power poles fell, and interstate highways were closed.

Warming Makes It Colder

Strange as it may seem, these events were as much a result of climate change (more commonly known as global warming just a few years back) as extreme heat, drought, and hurricanes. But the term *global warming* evokes images of heat waves and droughts, not bone-chilling cold. So when the extremely cold weather made headlines in March 2019, one of the most promi-

Monster Blizzards

When unusually severe cold weather hits, social media users often come up with nicknames that tend to stick. The blizzard that brought the northeastern United States to a standstill in 2010 earned the title Snowpocalypse. In January 2016 a record-setting East Coast blizzard was named Snowzilla, after the movie monster Godzilla. While the name might have provided some comic relief, the damage caused by the blizzard was anything but funny.

According to the Regional Snowfall Index used by the NOAA to assess winter storms, Snowzilla was rated a Category 5 "extreme" event in the Northeast and a Category 4 "crippling" event in the Southeast. The storm dumped 15 to 30 inches (38.1 to 76.2 cm) of snow on an area that stretched from Georgia to Massachusetts. Nearly 28 inches (71.1 cm) of snow fell in New York City in a single day, setting a record. The small town of Glengary, West Virginia, received 42 inches (107 cm) of snow. Wind gusts neared 40 miles per hour (64.4 kph) in places, creating blinding whiteout conditions. Around 103 million people in eleven states were affected by Snowzilla. At least fifty-five people were killed in incidents related to the storm. Economic losses were estimated at around $2.5 billion.

nent climate change deniers, then-president Donald Trump, took note. He tweeted this message: "In the beautiful Midwest, wind-chill temperatures are reaching minus 60 degrees, the coldest ever recorded. In coming days, expected to get even colder. People can't last outside even for minutes. What the hell is going on with Global Wa[r]ming? Please come back fast, we need you!"[37]

Those who mock the seriousness of climate change do not understand the science, experts say. The warming of the planet is the cause of extreme weather, both hot and cold. After the 2019 cold snap, atmospheric researchers at the Alfred Wegener Institute (AWI) in Bremerhaven, Germany, used artificial intelligence to study the phenomenon. The researchers showed that the jet stream was to blame for the unusually cold weather. The jet stream is powered by the temperature difference between the frigid air masses in the Arctic and the warmer air masses found further to the south. But this difference is shrinking as the Arctic warms. In 2019 the weakened jet stream coiled southward, pulling icy air that normally remains at the North Pole into Canada and the United States. This caused temperatures to crash to record lows. As AWI researcher Markus Rex explains, "Our findings confirm that the more frequently occurring cold phases in winter in the USA, Europe and Asia are by no means a contradiction to global warming; rather, they are a part of anthropogenic [human-caused] climate change."[38]

The unusually cold weather of early 2019 returned in November, when an Arctic air mass hit 240 million people living across the United States. Temperatures bottomed out at historic lows, and the cold triggered school closures throughout the Midwest, the mid-South, and the southern plains. While snow and cold are not unusual in November, the record low temperatures were blamed on intense warming in the Arctic Circle that pushed abnormally cold air south. According to atmospheric scientist Judah Cohen, "This Arctic outbreak is connected to the behavior of the jet stream and the polar vortex."[39]

With more Arctic air flowing south, North Americans can expect to see more extreme winter weather. But record-setting cold snaps and blinding blizzards will not be the only weather events caused by the faltering jet stream and warming polar vortex. A 2018 study by the publication *Science Advances* predicted that these changes will increase all manner of deadly weather events by as much as 50 percent by the end of the twenty-first century.

Cold in the Southern Hemisphere

The earth has two polar vortices, and the Antarctic vortex over the South Pole is the main weather maker for Australia and other regions at the bottom of the planet. The frigid air of the Antarctic polar vortex creates its own jet stream in the Southern Hemisphere. In this part of the world, the jet stream creates strong west-to-east winds called westerlies in Australia. As in the north, the strength of the Antarctic polar vortex effects the weather. When the vortex is strong, the cold air remains over the South Pole. When the vortex weakens, the jet stream buckles, pushing bitterly cold air north toward the equator. When winter comes to Australia (during the summer months in the Northern Hemisphere), this change in the Antarctic polar vortex can bring cold air and snow to a country that is usually hot and dry. These storms are referred to by Australians as polar blasts and polar plunges.

In May 2020 Australians shivered through their coldest polar plunge in decades. After experiencing the fifth-warmest April on record, the first day of May brought blizzard-like conditions to parts of southern Australia. In Sydney temperatures dipped to 14°F (-10°C) as strong winds uprooted trees and damaged buildings. The town of Falls Creek, New South Wales, saw a record snowfall of more than 3 feet (91.4 cm) that buried cars and disrupted travel.

The unusual cold continued through the month in the Southern Hemisphere. On May 28 fourteen low-temperature records were set in South Africa when a polar blast of Antarctic air pushed temperatures below freezing. The blast dumped snow in areas where most people have never seen the powdery white stuff.

Freezing Budding Trees

Many tree species are not equipped to deal with late-spring cold snaps like the one that hit the United States in May 2020. The natural cycle of these trees has been affected by climate change; the trees create leaves and flowers earlier than normal in the spring when the weather warms. This behavior, called "leaf out," is occurring about two weeks earlier on average than it has in past. But the earlier leaf out puts trees in danger during late-spring frosts because young leaves are vulnerable to freezing. When leaves freeze, they die, which can kill trees or stunt their growth.

Around fifteen hundred species are susceptible to late-spring frost damage, according to a comprehensive study by Swiss scientists published in the National Academy of Sciences journal *PNAS*. In one example cited by the study, a March cold snap in 2017 killed half the iconic cherry blossoms in Washington, DC. These blossoms emerged unusually early, in February, due to record-setting warm temperatures. In Europe the same weather conditions wiped out cultivated flowers and plants, which caused agricultural losses in the billions of dollars. Research shows that up to one-third of the trees in Europe and North America could be affected by similar problems.

Once again, a weakened, wavering jet stream was to blame for the unusual weather.

That same year, the first week in May saw spring-like temperatures in much of the United States—but then the polar vortex struck again. On May 9 a brutally cold air mass dipped down from the north, plunging the Midwest, South, and East back into winter. All-time May record lows were set in Indiana, Kentucky, New Jersey, New York, Tennessee, and elsewhere. It was 18°F (-7.8°C) in Van Wert, Ohio, the coldest May temperature in at least 127 years. Fort Wayne, Indiana, hit 23°F (-5°C), while thermometers dipped to 36°F (2.2°C) in New York City. There were strange May snowfalls in Albany, Detroit, and Pittsburgh. The cold weather killed spring flowers and damaged trees that were forming leaves earlier than usual due to the warm spring.

Extreme cold coming from the Arctic also created severe stresses on pipes, roads, and other infrastructure. During the winter blast of 2019, water mains froze in Chicago and Detroit,

leaving thousands without fresh water. City crews had to brave life-threatening weather to repair the damage. Natural gas supplies ran short in Minnesota and Michigan, where authorities asked residents to conserve energy by turning down their thermostats. Traffic was snarled by the snow, which caused thousands of car crashes.

Even as new records for heat are set almost every year, people can expect the frigid conditions to prevail at times. As atmospheric scientist Andrew Dessler says, "In a warming climate, you still expect to get extreme and sometimes record lows."[40]

Reversing Climate Change

The weather extremes seen in recent years are unusual in the history of earth's climate. Scientists have been able to determine that average global temperatures were very stable for at least the past ten thousand years as civilization developed. And until the late twentieth century, climate change seemed to be gradual, making it possible for policy makers and business leaders to ignore warnings issued by scientists. But in the twenty-first century, extreme weather events are making headlines on an almost daily basis. Hot days are getting much hotter; cold days are getting much colder. Massive storms are bringing unusually large amounts of rain and flooding. Hurricanes are reaching intensities never before seen. Droughts and wildfires are increasing in frequency and size. Scientists warn that these extreme weather events are likely to continue—and worsen—as climate change progresses. As astrophysicist Karel Schrijver and physician Iris Schrijver warn, "The atmosphere, the oceans, and the polar ice fields are . . . vast reservoirs of energy. . . . Once in motion, these [forces] are exceptionally hard to stop and reverse. It is like pushing a large ship or a heavy train: it takes much effort to get them moving, but once moving they have so much momentum that it is difficult to stop them."[41]

"In a warming climate, you still expect to get extreme and sometimes record lows occurring."[40]

—Andrew Dessler, atmospheric scientist

Slowing the momentum of climate change will take an unprecedented effort. Individuals, educational institutions, governments, and industries will have to work together to reduce production of greenhouse gases. The effort has been compared to fighting a world war, with battles taking place on many fronts. While the work will be difficult, there is no other choice if humanity—and the earth's delicate ecosystems—are to survive.

Introduction: The Climate Is Changing

1. Mark Schapiro, "In One Week in September, Nature Went Haywire," *Los Angeles Times*, October 18, 2020. www.latimes.com.
2. Jordan Thomas, "New Attacks on Climate Science," *Los Angeles Times*, October 14, 2020. https://edition.pagesuite.com.
3. Quoted in Jeff Masters, "September 2020 Was the Warmest September on Record, NOAA Reports," Yale Climate Connections, October 14, 2020. https://yaleclimateconnections.org.

Chapter 1: Intense Heat

4. Quoted in Anton Troianovski, "A Historic Heat Wave Roasts Siberia," *New York Times*, June 25, 2020. www.nytimes.com.
5. Quoted in Alejandra Borunda, "What a 100-Degree Day in Siberia Really Means," National Geographic, June 23, 2020. www.nationalgeographic.com.
6. Borunda, "What a 100-Degree Day in Siberia Really Means."
7. Quoted in Adrienne Arsht–Rockefeller Foundation Resilience Center, "Extreme Heat Resilience Alliance: Reducing Extreme Heat Risk for Vulnerable People," August 4, 2020. www.onebillionresilient.org.
8. Quoted in Science X, "Cooler for Parts of Europe, Spain Battles Wildfires," July 1, 2019. https://phys.org.
9. Brian Kahn, "A Potential Record Setting Heat Wave Is About to Scorch Europe," Gizmodo, June 24, 2019. https://earther.gizmodo.com.
10. *Science*, "The Hotter It Gets, the Hotter It Gets," August 3, 2006. www.sciencemag.org.
11. Quoted in Stephen Leahy, "Parts of Asia May Be Too Hot for People by 2100," National Geographic, August 2, 2017. www.nationalgeographic.com.

Chapter 2: Deadly Droughts and Gigafires

12. Quoted in Damien Cave, "Australia's Witnesses to Fire's Fury Are Desperate to Avoid a Sequel," *New York Times*, September 14, 2020. www.nytimes.com.
13. Quoted in Linda Givetash, "Australian Wildfires Declared Among the 'Worst Wildlife Disasters in Modern History,'" NBC News, July 28, 2020. www.nbcnews.com.
14. David Wallace-Wells, "California Has Australian Problems Now," *New York*, August 21, 2020. https://nymag.com.
15. Quoted in Hillary Rosner, "A Tiny Pest Helped Stoke This Year's Devastating Wildfires," National Geographic, October 1, 2020. www.nationalgeographic.com.
16. Quoted in Bettina Boxall, "Sequoias Fall to Giant-Killer," *Los Angeles Times*, November 16, 2020. https://edition.page suite.com.
17. Quoted in Amy McKeever, "Fire Clouds and Fire Tornadoes: How Wildfires Spawn Extreme Weather," National Geographic, September 24, 2020. www.nationalgeographic.com.
18. Quoted in Blacki Migliozzi et al., "Record Wildfires on the West Coast Are Capping a Disastrous Decade," *New York Times*, September 24, 2020. www.nytimes.com.
19. Wallace-Wells, "California Has Australian Problems Now."

Chapter 3: Record Rainstorms and Flooding

20. Exodus 10:4–5 (New International Version).
21. Madeleine Stone, "A Plague of Locusts Has Descended on East Africa. Climate Change May Be to Blame," National Geographic, February 14, 2020. www.nationalgeographic.com.
22. Quoted in Pranav Baskar, "Locusts Are a Plague of Biblical Scope 2020. Why? And . . . What Are They Exactly?," NPR, June 14, 2020. www.npr.org.
23. Richard Munang, "Locust Swarms and Climate Change," United Nations Environment Programme, February 6, 2020. www.unenvironment.org.
24. Quoted in Sarah Almukhtar et al., "The Great Flood of 2019: A Complete Picture of a Slow-Motion Disaster," *New York Times*, September 11, 2019. www.nytimes.com.

25. Quoted in Chris Machian, "Record Snowfall, 'Historic' Bomb Cyclone Are Forces Behind Nebraska Floods, Blizzard," *Omaha (NE) World-Herald*, March 17, 2020. https://omaha.com.
26. Quoted in Jason Samenow and Jeff Halverson, "How a Stalled Storm over Baltimore Unleased Flooding Rain and 70 MPH Winds Tuesday," *Washington Post*, August 7, 2019. www.washingtonpost.com.
27. Vaishnavi Chandrashekhar, "As the Monsoon and Climate Shift, India Faces Worsening Floods," Yale Environment 360, September 17, 2019. https://e360.yale.edu.
28. Quoted in Connie Kuntz, "'Too Hot, Too Cold, Too Wet, Too Dry'—an Illinois Farmer's Take on This Year's Harvest," WNIU, October 20, 2020. www.northernpublicradio.org.

Chapter 4: Monster Hurricanes

29. Matthew Cappucci, "Two Category 4 Hurricanes Hit the Same Place in Two Weeks. That's Unheard Of," *Washington Post*, November 17, 2020. www.washingtonpost.com.
30. Alejandra Borunda, "Tropical Storms Can Sometimes 'Supercharge' the Storms That Follow," National Geographic, October 9, 2020. www.nationalgeographic.com.
31. Quoted in Brian Kahn, "Superstorm Sandy and Sea Level Rise," NOAA Climate.gov, November 5, 2012. www.climate.gov.
32. Quoted in Robinson Meyer, "Hurricane Florence's Slow Speed Is Ominous," *The Atlantic*, September 12, 2018. www.theatlantic.com.
33. Jeff Masters, "Super Typhoon Goni Slams into Philippines as Strongest Landfall Tropical Cyclone on Record," Yale Climate Connections, November 1, 2020. https://yaleclimateconnections.org.

Chapter 5: Deadly Cold and Snow

34. Quoted in Angela Fritz, "Midwest Temperatures 'Could Approach All-Time Record Values' Wednesday Night," *Washington Post*, January 30, 2019. www.washingtonpost.com.

35. Quoted in Fritz, "Midwest Temperatures 'Could Approach All-Time Record Values' Wednesday Night."
36. Quoted in Brian Resnick and Kainaz Amaria, "What -20° Looks like in the Polar Vortex Across the Midwest," Vox, January 30, 2019. www.vox.com.
37. Quoted in Chris Mooney and Brady Dennis, "Trump Always Dismisses Climate Change When It's Cold. Not So Fast, Experts Say," *Washington Post*, January 29, 2019. www.washingtonpost.com.
38. Quoted in ScienceDaily, "A Warming Arctic Produces Weather Extremes in Our Latitudes," May 28, 2019. www.sciencedaily.com.
39. Quoted in Alejandra Borunda, "Snow in Texas and Ice in Alabama? Unusual Cold Weather Could Become More Common," National Geographic, November 13, 2019. www.nationalgeographic.com.
40. Quoted in Mooney and Dennis, "Trump Always Dismisses Climate Change When It's Cold."
41. Karel Schrijver and Iris Schrijver, *Living with the Stars.* New York: Oxford University Press, 2015, pp. 101–3.

ORGANIZATIONS AND WEBSITES

Climate Reality Project
www.climaterealityproject.org

The Climate Reality Project was founded by former vice president Al Gore to mobilize over nineteen thousand climate reality leaders, who push for practical clean energy policies across the United States and elsewhere.

Earth Guardians
www.earthguardians.org

Earth Guardians is a student organization made up of activists, artists, and musicians dedicated to empowering young people to take over as leaders of the environmental movement. The group's website features inclusive information about environmental issues and ongoing campaigns.

Earth Island Institute
www.earthisland.org

The Earth Island Institute was founded in 1982 to support activism around environmental issues. The group provides financial sponsorship to young environmental leaders who are searching for solutions to the climate crisis.

Environmental Defense Fund (EDF)
www.edf.org

The EDF was founded in 1967 to fight against the use of the pesticide DDT. Today the group is working to stabilize the climate, save ecosystems, and ensure environmental justice for the poor.

Global Forest Watch

www.globalforestwatch.org

This website monitors forests throughout the world with maps of wildfires, deforestation, and illegal logging using satellite imagery, news articles, and other real-time information.

NASA Earth Observatory

https://earthobservatory.nasa.gov

This US space agency website features time-lapse satellite maps that show wildfires, hurricanes, and other extreme weather events in real time in Australia, the Sierra Nevada mountain range in the western United States, and elsewhere.

Natural Resources Defense Council (NRDC)

https://act.nrdc.org

With more than 3 million members, the NRDC is one of the leading environmental organizations in the world. The council's website provides wide-ranging environmental information about climate change, biodiversity, forests, and oceans.

350.org

https://350.org

This group founded by environmental author Bill McKibben is focused on reducing the amount of CO_2 in the environment. The website provides a resource guide for organizers that includes presentations, photos, icons, and templates.

FOR FURTHER RESEARCH

Books

Craig E. Blohm, *What Is the Impact of Climate Change?* San Diego: ReferencePoint, 2020.

Bill Gates, *How to Avoid Climate Disaster: The Solutions We Have and the Breakthroughs We Need*. New York: Knopf, 2021.

Karen Bush Gibson, *Meteorology: Cool Women Who Weather Storms*. White River Junction, VT: Nomad, 2020.

Joshua Sneideman and Erin Twamley, *Climate Change: The Science Behind Melting Glaciers and Warming Oceans with Hands-On Science Activities*. White River Junction, VT: Nomad, 2020.

Diane C. Taylor, *The Science of Natural Disasters: When Nature and Humans Collide*. White River Junction, VT: Nomad, 2020.

Greta Thunberg, *No One Is Too Small to Make a Difference*. New York: Penguin, 2019.

Internet Sources

Alejandra Borunda, "What a 100-Degree Day in Siberia Really Means," National Geographic, June 23, 2020. www.nationalgeographic.com.

Vaishnavi Chandrashekhar, "As the Monsoon and Climate Shift, India Faces Worsening Floods," Yale Environment 360, September 17, 2019. https://e360.yale.edu.

Stephen Leahy, "Parts of Asia May Be Too Hot for People by 2100," National Geographic, August 2, 2017. www.nationalgeographic.com.

Jeff Masters, "September 2020 Was the Warmest September on Record, NOAA Reports," Yale Climate Connections, October 14, 2020. https://yaleclimateconnections.org.

Jordan Thomas, "Op-Ed: The New Line of Attack on Climate Science in the Age of Megafires," *Los Angeles Times*, October 14, 2020. www.latimes.com.

David Wallace-Wells, "California Has Australian Problems Now," *New York*, August 21, 2020. https://nymag.com.

INDEX